Life Problems

Life Problems

Rev. G. CAMPBELL MORGAN

BAKER BOOK HOUSE
Grand Rapids, Michigan

Reprinted 1978 by
Baker Book House
from the edition issued in 1899
by Fleming H. Revell Company

ISBN: 0-8010-6056-7

Second printing, May 1980

PHOTOLITHOPRINTED BY CUSHING - MALLOY, INC.
ANN ARBOR, MICHIGAN, UNITED STATES OF AMERICA

Contents

I
SELF

"When I consider Thy heavens, the work of Thy fingers, the moon and the stars which Thou hast ordained: What is man that Thou art mindful of him, and the son of man that Thou visitest him?"— PSALM viii. 3, 4.

I

SELF

In the second of these verses the writer enunciates the first great problem of every human life, and it is a problem which encompasses all others. The old philosophers and teachers summed up their philosophy and teaching in that one phrase, "Man, know thyself." And if man can but know himself, there will be no problem that he has not solved. When man truly knows himself, and has unravelled the mysteries of his own existence, and fathomed all the deeps of his own being, then, surely, he will also have discovered God, the Creator and Sustainer.

By that knowledge of himself, he will have learned also the problem of his brother-man, and so have entered into the realization of the great brotherhood of humanity. By that knowledge of himself, and of the possibilities of his nature, he will have come to understand that strange, almost meaningless expression, so often upon our lips, and so little understood, "Eternity." When man knows himself, then he will have discovered also the secrets of nature, and will be at home amid all their varied and varying avenues. Tennyson sang truly—

> " Flower in the crannied wall,
>   I pluck you out of the cranny;
>   Hold you here in my hand,
> Little flower, root and all —
>   And if I could understand
> What you are, root and all, and all in all,
>   I should know what God and man is."

And therefore it is that I repeat: The first problem that faces the thinking mind is the problem of Self. Who am I? What am I? Whence came I? Whither go I? What mean these strange conflicting elements within my nature? How is it that one day I love, and within an hour I hate? What is the meaning of all these strange contradictory ex-

periences as I take my way through
life?

Our present consideration is confined
within very narrow limits. We shall
endeavor to answer the psalmist's question, "What is man?" in the light of
the New Testament revelation. "What
is man?"—not, What is man, blighted,
dwarfed, broken, sin-stained, as we
know him? That will be a subject for
future consideration; but what is man
in himself—what is the Divine ideal?
When, far away in the past, God said,
in that Eternal Counsel of His own being,
"Let us make man," what had He in
His thought and on His heart? "What
is man?" In order that we may understand the problem as it presents itself to-
day, it is absolutely necessary that we
get further back in the question, and ask
the original intention and meaning of
the creation of man. I cannot understand fallen man, sinful and heart-
broken, save as I have the vision of man
unfallen, without sin, whole in heart
and affection toward God. "What is

man?" For the sake of the youngest reader, let me take the simplest illustration. Were I a stranger to this land, and were I suddenly brought here from some of the dark places of the earth, did I know nothing of civilization, naught of all the progress of this rapidly fading century, and were I placed first of all in connection with our great railway system on some point where an hour before there had been a fearful wreck, would it be fair to say to me as I gazed upon the wreck of the locomotive and train scattered in confusion, "That is a train"? Every child will see how absurd it would be. That is the wreckage, the result of the accident, and it is the very splendor of the construction that has made that wreckage so profound and appalling. If I want to know what a train is, I must find out before the accident. "What is man?" It is not fair to point to man as you see him to-day, with the blemish and blight of sin upon him; with the dimness of sin in his eye, and the weariness of sin in his physical frame; with his mental vigor enfeebled, and spiritual power benumbed.

"What is man?" That is the question; and in order to answer it, I must get behind the present condition of affairs, and come to understand what man is in himself, so far as the thought and intention of God are concerned. We shall therefore, *in the first place*, consider the problem as stated; and *secondly*, we shall direct our attention to a close inspection of that problem; and *thirdly and lastly*, we shall endeavor to apply that problem to personal consciousness.

I

First of all, will you notice the psalmist's statement of the problem, because it is full of interest. He approaches his question from certain points of observation, and it is only as we understand these points that we shall gather the full force and meaning of his question.

You notice what his first observation is. "When I consider Thy heavens, the work of Thy fingers, the moon and the stars which Thou has ordained: What is man?" The second observation, "Thou art mindful of man, Thou visitest him." "What is man?" Take these two points of vision for a moment and look at them closely. "When I consider Thy heavens"—and I suppose the psalmist had a right to say that. I suppose he had considered God's heavens. I do not deem that very many of us would have any right to make use of those words as our own. There may be here one, and there another, who have considered the heavens. We have all, in some of those old moments of simplicity—childhood's moments—gone outside the door and gazed some night at the star-bespangled heavens. And we have in those days— some of you have almost forgotten them —felt the thrill, the awe, and the impressiveness of the silent eloquence of the night. "When I consider Thy heavens" in their countless numbers, in their perfect order, in their absolute freedom—so far as man has ever been able to detect— from conflicting interests, in the infinite music of the spheres that stretch beyond my ken; "When I consider Thy heavens," not only in their essential wonder, but "When I consider Thy heavens, the work of Thy fingers, the moon and the stars which Thou hast ordained: what is man?"

And the answer comes clearly to every heart as the question is proposed. Man is small, frail, vanishing; and we answer the psalmist's question in his own language, from another of his psalms, "Surely man at his best estate is altogether vanity."

Man comes and goes, a bubble on the stream, on which for a few passing moments the lights and shadows play; and then he is "forgotten, as a dream dies at the opening day." The stars upon which we look to-day are the self-same orbs of light upon which our savage forefathers gazed. But men have come and gone in quick succession, until it seems as if the cold stars upon the plain of heaven have laughed at man in his going and coming. I stand at the foot of the mountain which lifts its head beyond the cloud, and catches on its summit the first gleam of the king of day in his rising, and I say, "What am I?" That mountain has been there through the passing of the ages, and I am here and shall be gone before the sun melts the snow upon its summit. "What is man?"

But the psalmist has another point of observation. "Thou art mindful of him; Thou visitest him." If the heavens are wonderful, they are the "work of Thy fingers." The extremities of Divine power have done these things, but Thou Thyself art mindful of man. Thou hast manipulated the orbs of night, and the procession of the centuries without effort, without weariness, without journeying; but Thou visitest *him*. "What is man?" Frail, insignificant, vanishing, laughed at by material grandeur, and yet attracting God, so that the Eternal is "mindful of him and visits him."

Thus the problem is stated; and I want you to see very clearly how close is the connection between these two points of observation, and how, moreover, had there not been two points of observation, the wonder never would have been. If man were obviously greater than the universe, surely, then, he is equal with God; and I am not surprised God is "mindful of him and visits him." On the other hand, if God does not visit this man, then I ask no question about him. He is part of the perishing around me. He lives his little life, and has his day, and is lost, so far as identity and personality are concerned. He returns to Mother Earth, and mixes again with the first elements that have composed him for a few passing years, and we shall never know him again. If that be so I ask no question. He is the fairest flower that has blossomed on the earth; the most blessed form of materialism that any have ever seen, and that is all: but when I see him frailer than matter, weaker than the mountains, smaller than the stars, vanishing in the presence of the fastnesses of nature, and yet God visits him, and is mindful of him (and to min-

gle the sweet music of the Old and New
Testaments, God puts his tears into His
bottle, numbers the hairs of his head,
directs his steps), then have I to wonder, and am constrained to ask with the
psalmist of old, "What is man?"

This statement of the problem is necessary in order to arrest the careless and
indifferent who are taking their own life
and being for granted, as something
purely accidental. Let us face this twofold vision and its problem—less than
stars and systems, and suns, and order,
and yet such that attracts God, so that
He is mindful of and visits him. "What
is man?"

II

Now I propose finding my definition
in the New Testament, and I shall only
trouble you to look at it in order to remember the phrase. In Paul's first letter
to the Thessalonians, in the last chapter
and the 23d verse, he makes use of a
phrase of infinite meaning, as I believe,
giving us in his own clear, lucid way a

definition which answers the question
propounded in this psalm of olden times
—"The God of peace sanctify you
wholly"; and then he proceeds to give
us an exposition of his own phrase
"wholly." What does he mean when
he says that sanctification has to be
wholly complete? "May your spirit,
soul, and body be preserved entire, without blame, unto the coming of our Lord
Jesus Christ." I am not discussing this
text; I am simply lifting out of it—in
order that we may study the problem
that faces us—that one phrase, "your
spirit, soul, and body." And upon this
occasion the original words are used
most carefully; and that is why I take
this phrase and ask you to look at it
for a moment or two. Spirit, soul, and
body. That is man. Shall we take each
of these and consider them briefly, only
for the purpose of our argument; and
that we may follow the line of thought
we shall not take them in the apostle's
order, but we shall, reversing the order,
take first body, then soul, and then spirit.

BODY. "What is man?" We have too long answered the question carelessly, and have said body and soul, and too long been misusing a word by talking about saving the soul. Now what a man needs to have saved in that evangelical sense of the word, is not the *soul*, but the *spirit*. Let the *spirit* be regenerated, and then soul and body alike are saved; but it is important that we should look at this vision and consider these words—body, soul, and spirit. The body is of the earth, and therefore earthy, and yet it is the highest form of earth-life. Let us be very simple and childlike as we think about that lowest form of human personality—physical power. It was the psalmist who said we are "fearfully and wonderfully made," and yet how few of us realize that that is true; how few have set themselves, quietly and thoughtfully, to think of the marvellous and matchless mechanism of their own frames! This is the day of invention and of progress, when man is engaged in a continuous whirl of discovery; and according to the very latest book by Mr. Bellamy, "Equality," the time is coming when we shall not work, but press a button and everything will be done for us. May I be dead before the day comes! That is all I wish. But we are discovering everywhere, and men are perpetually inventing new forms of machinery. But the mechanism of my hand has never been equalized in the dream of any inventor; and what is true of me is true of every one. Take the hand, and you will find that the thumb faces every finger so that I can pick from the ground the smallest thing that my hand can lift, and also grasp the lever that moves great masses of matter.

You remember when you had those first visions of physiology that so entranced some of you that you never left the study, and finally mastered it, and entered upon a profession that has served humanity and is always an adornment. Some saw the vision and were afraid, and drew back. Think of it for a moment, the body of man, and remember

there is no flower that blossoms upon
the sod so fair; no tree that grows in
the wood so wondrous in its powers of
endurance. "Oh," but you say, "there
are trees growing to-day that were old
when we began to be"; but they have
never faced such storms as you have.
All the wind that blows, the rain that
splashes, and the changes of atmosphere
that tell upon the oak, are child's play
compared to the mental anguish and
heart-break that have swept across your
life; and yet you have endured. With
God a thousand years are as a day; and
with man, as compared to the oak, a
thousand years are as a day. One day
has in it of force and meaning more
than all the life the plant or the tree lives
in its long succession of the seasons. So
if you think of the material side of man's
existence, he is more wonderful in his
strength, as in his beauty, than anything
else God has made. And yet what is
this frame of mine ? It is the carbon
upon which the light of God is to play
and have its work. As is the carbon to

the electric light, so is the body of man
to the spirit of man. Only that, nothing
more! It is the basis of life, that upon
which the rest manifests itself for the
time being, and only for the time being.
This body of mine, surpassing in its
wonder all human understanding, is for
to-day, not to-morrow. In God's great
to-morrow, I must have a body of another form—no longer the earthly and
material, but the heavenly and the spiritual. This is the tabernacle for the spirit
in the day of its probation. More marvellous in its mechanism, as we have
said, than sun, stars, tree, or plant, or
any other form of matter; and yet being
but the lowest stratum in the complex
life of man.

Soul.—This word "soul"—the Greek
word—is a word that always refers to
the animal life of man, the conscious
force, that within which feels pain or joy.
You will agree that the animal life in
man far exceeds, in every way, all other
forms of animal life. Remember that
man, as an animal, without any reference

to the great crowning glory, is capable of art, and music, and literature, and imagination. All these things may flourish even though a man be spiritually dead. I want to save that phrase now, because it is on your mind. I may forget to correct it. Some one says, "Do you mean to say that these may all find full play in an unspiritual man?" By no means. I say the best art the world has ever known has been inspired, and under the dominion of spirit. The finest poetry that men have ever penned has been written when the life was under the dominion of the highest form of its complex nature—spirit. But this I do say, within the mental range of the soul life there may be art, music, literature, and imagination, all the while the spirit of man is dead in trespasses and sins. This is no new story or theory. If you trace your way back to Genesis you will find how Enoch was the seventh from Adam through Seth; and of Enoch it was said, "he walked with God." Lamech lived about the same time, he being the seventh from

Adam through Cain; and you study his times and find how there was industry, and art, and the enfranchisement of woman—all without God. And that old story has been repeated ever since. A man can be an artist, a poet, a literary genius, a messenger to his fellow-men on high moral lines, even though the spirit is dead. But, so far, we have only touched upon the body and soul. What next?

SPIRIT.—That which is divine; the free breath of God. Divine in its possibilities and powers, the supreme glory of every human life, unheard of by any form of lower life than man—the spirit. If I meet a man in the road, I meet first of all his bodily presence. That appeals to me through the avenue of my sight. But when presently we pause and hold converse, I reach his soul—the mental side of the man—through the avenue of his speech; but when I have lived with him and tabernacled with him, I shall reach, if it be alive and prospering there, his spirit, not through the avenue of sight or speech, but through the avenue of the influence he will exert upon me. Thus the easiest thing which I can come in contact with is his body, the physical side of his nature, fearful, wonderful, majestic. More difficult to realize is *brotherhood* in the region of the mind; but most subtle and hard to reach is the kindred touch of spirit that is the crowning glory of every human being. What is man? Less than the heavens, and yet so wondrous in himself that God is mindful of him and visits him. Man is body—of the earth; he is soul—the highest form of animal life; he is spirit—offspring of God, created not only by Him, but in His image.

"What is man?" He is the union of the spiritual and the material. He is the crown of all nature, and in man nature blossoms into God. You may have your evolutionary theory at this point, if you like; you may take your lowest form of life back to what scientists speak of as protoplasm. Ruskin said it would spoil a good deal of the scientific aspect of things if the words of the teachers were explained. Protoplasm means, "first stuck together." It may be well to remember that. Go back to them, because I should like to know what was stuck together, and who stuck them. But get back to your "first stuck together," and watch it upward, if you like. I am not going to quarrel with it. I don't know enough to say whether it is true; but whether it is true or not, one thing is certain, that behind all is God. Let me travel up through every point of beauty, growing grander and grander until it is lost in man, and in man all nature touches God. For in man there is the Divine spark, the Divine nature; and every man, woman, and child is a part of God, created in His image, and touched with His life and spirit. Nature touches God nowhere but in man, in that sense there is nothing of the Divine on the earth save man; and in the heaven that lies above us and the light that is beyond the shadow, there is nothing, so far as we know, of earth but man. So man becomes the strangest and grandest of the works of God, in his own being marrying earth and heaven, linking matter to spirit, and being in himself at once of the earth and of the heavens—the strangest and most marvellous combination of the skill and work of the Divine.

If man sin, then all nature will go down with him, trees, and flowers—on all will be the chill of man's sin. Well does the writer of the New Testament say that "the whole creation groaneth and travaileth together in pain until now." Then, when spirit is dominant in man, he is at his best. Spirit is supreme; and soul and body are subservient to spirit. And when spirit is supreme, man has dominion, as the psalmist says, and the writer of the Hebrews repeats "over all things."

Then if man be spirit in his complex and essential being, he is immortal, and there is no death. "Oh," you say, "but there is death. Men have died through all the ages." My friends, that is not a part of our study. "What is man?" I do not ask what he is in his fall. Remember, "the wages of sin is death." Death came in because of sin in man himself; in the essential glory of the Divine creation there is no death, transition rather. This life is a probation, a time of testing and trial, in which all the magnificence of his own being comes before his own vision. Then, when the testing time is over, and the work is done, comes the change—the transition, that leaves behind the process of probation, and takes up new work in the Kingdom of the Eternal, fulfilling the purpose of God, and stepping out to unknown regions of which man in all his dreams can say nothing, for God has hidden these things. "What is man?" Body, soul, and spirit.

III

What is my personal consciousness, in view of such a study? I am not what I have described.

That is not the story of my life. Well, that is precisely what the writer of the

letter to the Hebrews teaches. He quotes
the psalm from which our text is taken.
"What is man that Thou art mindful of
him, and visitest him ?" and then he declares, "We see not yet all things put
under his feet."   I pray you notice that
it does not in the first place mean the
feet of Jesus; the writer is speaking of
man—"Now we see not all things subjected to him"—all things are not yet
subjected to man—"but we see Jesus,
Who was made a little lower than the
angels for the suffering of death,
crowned."   Oh, if I could put into that
all the music it contains! We have
looked at the vision, and we are not that
which has been described.   But we see
"Jesus, Who has been made a little
lower than the angels," come to our
level—and how do we see Him ?
Crowned.   Then there is one Man to
whom all things have been put in subjection; one Man Who has fulfilled His
Divine ideal; one Man in the presence of
the Eternal God Who is there, not by the
right of pardon purchased for Him, but

by the right of His own strong, pure
life.

We do not see all things put in subjection to man; but we see Jesus crowned.
And why is He crowned? Will you hear
those closing words of that same most
wonderful chapter, 8th verse, "Thou
hast put all things in subjection under
His feet;" and then on to the 18th verse,
"For in that He Himself hath suffered,
being tempted, He is able to succor
them that are tempted." He is crowned.
And because He is crowned He is able to
bring the power of His own resurrection
life into my life. He is able to take me,
wreck as I am, ruined as I am, failure as
I am, and by discipline remould and re-
make me out of the wreckage of my sin.
"He is able to save to the uttermost
those who come unto God by Him."
My possibility: Man—body, soul, and
spirit. My failure: I have sinned. My
possession in Christ: He is able to succor.

Now I would like to say solemnly, in
conclusion, and leave the question in all

its simplicity—On which plane of life are you living—body, soul, or spirit? The great crowd of men to-day are living on the lowest; but a large number are living on the second—soul, mental culture—and thank God, there are those who are living on the third—spirit. That is the supreme thing. Where dost thou live, my brother? For bodily satisfaction, or mental culture, or spiritual growth? For only as thou livest on the third and greatest, can the others be all that they may be, and all that is God's will that they should be. If hitherto thou hast lived in the realm of the physical, the fleshly, the carnal, the material, I call you in the name of the "crowned Man" Who is able to "succor you who are tempted" to His Cross, and to His side, and to His Kingdom.

II

ENVIRONMENT

"For in Him we live, and move, and have our being."
ACTS xvii. 28.

II

WE have considered the problem of Self. We now turn to the consideration of the forces which affect a man from without—his environment. We shall deal with Environment, firstly, as a popular conception; secondly, as a Divine revelation; and then we shall discuss the relation of these two views.

I

Primarily, let us take the popular idea —an idea based upon facts which are patent to all observers, and evident to every one of us, not merely from our observation of the lives of others, but from our own experience.

Man is acted upon and changed by the everyday surroundings of his life. This is seen in a striking way in the effect produced upon a man by the company with which he associates. If that company is refined and cultured, he will, almost in spite of himself, become in some measure refined. If, on the other hand, a man, born in refined life, choose to make companions of the debased, sordid, and brutal, he will undoubtedly weave into his own character those elements of baseness, sordidness, and brutality. Every man is made, in some measure, by the company he keeps.

Again, a man's character is moulded, imperceptibly to himself it may be, but most surely, by his daily occupation. There are some people more clever than others, who profess to be able to tell you to what profession a man belongs as they look at him in the street. There certainly are men who carry the profession they follow stamped on their face and marked in their bearing. I am not, however, speaking so much of what can be seen on the surface, as of the deep inner reality of the case; and I say that a man is very largely moulded in character by his occupation. Is was my lot, some years ago, to conduct a Mission at Crewe, where those magnificent locomotives of the North-Western Railway Company are built; and there for fourteen days I came into contact, for the most part, with men who worked in those shops. It was a remarkable fact that these men were not prepared to take for granted any single thing I said. Neither were they prepared to accept an ideal of life simply because it was the ideal of another man. With hard-headed shrewdness they followed me as I dealt with them; and not until they were clearly convinced of the reasonableness of the plan of salvation, and of its actual suitability to their known needs, were they prepared to make any confession of faith. These men spent six days of the week in doing work that could not be loosely performed. Every small piece of the machinery of those majestic engines had perfectly to complement and fit its neighbor. There was exactitude in these men's lives for six days, and when they began to touch spiritual verities they brought to their study the same precision of observation that they applied to the work that their hands undertook. They were moulded mentally by their occupation.

In 1896 I stood in one of the great slaughter-yards of Chicago; and as I looked at things which I do not propose to describe to you, I felt that no man could work perpetually in this atmosphere without being brutalized; and I was told afterward that there were justices in that neighborhood who had declined to take the evidence of some of these men when they knew their employment. A man is moulded and made by his occupation.

You will agree with me that a man's character is moulded and fashioned by his reading. Men and women make or mar their lives by the books they read in their spare time. Literature that is frothy, sensational, light, will create character that is frothy, sensational, light. On the other hand, a book of solid thought and set purpose—a book that cannot be taken up flippantly for five minutes now and then, but arrests the kingly quality of mental power, and demands undivided attention—will produce character that is strong, true, and abiding.

It is indisputable also that a man is made or marred by the place of his abode. The man who lives in the tenement-house or the slum is of necessity a widely different character from the man who is born in the cottage on the hillside, amid the clustering roses and trailing honeysuckle, and the sweetness of the garden with all fragrant herbs.

Thus all through life man is being influenced by his surroundings.

Out of these facts certain teachers have been deducing a philosophy of life which, at the first blush, seems to be plausible, possible, and even probable. That philosophy may thus be stated:—If a man is influenced by his surroundings, all you have to do to effect the transformation of the man is to re-make them. Remove the man out of a slum to a model dwelling in

the country or the suburbs; take him out
of his workshop—which is a veritable
death-trap on account of its unhealthy
conditions—and put him into one that is
well ventilated with all modern appli-
ances, and the atmosphere of which is
pure and sweet; take him away from
the neighborhood where crime is ram-
pant, and plant him among the green
fields; hang a few pictures on the walls
of his house; supply him with a bath;
and you will re-make the man. That is
the popular doctrine of environment.

It has been said that the doctrine of
environment was smashed to pieces in
the Garden of Eden; and it is perfectly
true. God did not start man in a fac-
tory, or a tenement-house, or a slum; He
started him in a garden where there was
the most perfect environment for all his
complex nature; for physical life is ever
at its best in the country, though we say
it who live amid the grime and toil of
the city. Surely mental vigor has ever
been most perfectly developed when it
has escaped from the restless crowd to

the loneliness of mountains and forests, and has dwelt "near to Nature's heart." I think it is much easier to pray under the blue, and the trees on the green-sward, than where the houses congregate so thickly that your vision of Nature is limited; and you forget the blue, and the tree, and the green. In this perfect environment of the garden God put man, without hereditary taint; and yet he failed.

We need not go so far back as the Garden of Eden, but come to later times; and, out of Bible history, take one man who started his life with environment more complete than that of any other man; who had his kingdom prepared for him by the heroic warrior-spirit of his father, and who entered, not only upon the kingdom so prepared, but upon the heritage of his father's penitence and tears; a man who came to the building of the House of God, prompted by High Heaven, and took up a work which his father had not been allowed to touch on account of the failure in his life. What

splendid opportunities for the develop-
ment of an unique personality; and yet I
have no hesitation in asserting that of all
the miserable failures recorded in the
Book of Truth, no failure was ever more
miserable or complete than that of Solomon.   Perfect environment was not sufficient.

When, in this country, our politicians
and thinkers were facing the great problems of educating the people, it was the
Iron Duke, a man of stern will, the hero
of many a hard-fought battle, and yet a
man of keen perception, who said,
" Gentlemen, if you are only going to
educate the children, .you are only going
to make them clever devils."   And what
he said was true.   The whole history of
man proves that environment is not sufficient.   If you take a man from the slum
and put him in the suburb, he will, unless you touch him in the very centre of
his being with some marvellous regenera-
tive force, by his very presence in the
suburb degrade it to the level of the slum.
So that the popular doctrine of environ-

ment is one which experience has proved to be futile.

II

We turn to our second consideration, that of Environment as a Divine revelation. We have it in our text, "In Him we live, and move, and have our being." If that teach us anything, it teaches us that every human being has the living God as true environment. Now we are face to face with something that is so familiar, that it has lost its power to touch and move our hearts. No one will quarrel with that statement; and, believe me, the most difficult task is to get people to believe the things they think they do believe. If you make an announcement that will challenge men's credulity, they are aroused to attention; but if you tell them the things in which they believe, they go away unbelieving, simply because of their familiarity.

"In Him we live, and move, and have our being." Then our first environment is God. "In Him we live." What is life? None can tell. Life is a perpetual mystery that baffles the thinkers and scientists of every age. Whether you take the life of plant, or animal, or the higher life of man, you are still in the presence of mystery. No man has ever seen life, or been able to analyze it. A scientific observer sat for long and weary years in his laboratory in Germany, taking the component parts of man's material nature and endeavoring to combine these parts so as to produce life; but he failed. You stand by the bedside of a dying man. He is alive: he is dead. What has happened? None can solve the riddle. No one saw pass away from him the principle that made the difference between clay and humanity.

While our text does not give us final and detailed explanation of this problem of life, it declares a great principle concerning it. "In Him we live"—that which is life, that which differentiates between us who live, and the dead bodies that wait for burial in our city, is that which is in God. It is "in Him we live." Then, to bring that great essential truth more closely to our notice, the apostles write, "In Him we live, *and move*." No hand is uplifted save under Divine energy; no step is taken except in the power of God. We have found our way from various homes and various circumstances into this House of Prayer, and the energy that has brought us here —very little as it seemed in its distribution among the units, but enormous in its mass—was the energy of God. And then again, repeating the whole fact, he adds, "and have our being." Then the first environment, the nearest fact, the supreme truth in every life is "GOD." All other environment is false and partial, and therefore does not touch the man himself.

Falling back for a moment upon our first study in this series, think of man at his best, with the body kept under in its proper place; that is to say, physical and mental life-power subservient to the spirit. When spirit dominates, what then? Then God is conscious environment, and everything else in man answers that first influence. It is in God that man lives, and moves, and has his being; and so, nearer to him than the book he reads, than the house in which he dwells, than the occupation of all the days, than the companions of his life— nearer than all is God. It is in "Him man lives, and moves, and has his being."

As we have combatted the false deduction that is made from the ordinary statement of environment, we now proceed to make a true deduction from this Divine relation. The man who consciously abides in God is superior to every other environment, master of every other force that comes against his life. The man in the slum, what shall we do with him? Take him out of it? No; we will lead him by the way of the Cross into living communion with God. He will re-make the man, and within a very few days or weeks he will change his own environment by moving from the slum somewhere else. The man whose work and reading and all his nature is tending to degrade and debase him—what shall we do with him? Begin with the environment? No; begin with the man. Restore him to right relationship with the Omnipotent, the Omnipresent, and the Omniscient. Let him, not merely as a dead theory, but as a living fact, "live, and move, and have his being in God," and with all-conquering might he will put the foot of his manhood upon the neck of every adversary from without, and will re-make all his environment in that Divine strength.

The law of environment still holds, but there is a higher law of environment; and when man obeys the higher law, all the lower laws become subservient, and contribute, not to his disaster and defeat, but to his making.

May we reverently take as our supreme example of that fact the one perfect Man, our adorable Redeemer, and compare Him with the man of Old Testament history whom we have mentioned. One would hardly care to compare Jesus with Solomon, were it not that Jesus did so

Himself. "A greater than Solomon is here." Now mark the difference in this particular consideration. Solomon started, as we have said, in perfect environment, and he failed. Think, if you will, of the environment of the life of Jesus Christ from the standpoint of His peculiar mission to the world, and you will see that from first to last everything, humanly speaking, was against Him. A man of the people, born a peasant, and all through life suffering poverty—and poverty then, as now, was a crime in the eye of the crowd. When He gathered His own disciples round Him they never understood Him; and in the critical, tragical moment of His life, they all forsook Him and fled.

Solomon, through perfect environment, comes to the days of shadow; and listen, he gives you the story of his failure: "Vanity of vanities, all is vanity, saith the preacher." Jesus comes to the close of His sojourn on the earth, and what does He say? "All authority is given unto Me, in heaven and in earth." Con-

trast the two statements: "Vanity of
vanities." "All authority given to Him."
The former is the language of a man
who through his own sin lost the sense
of his true environment, and so became
the slave of all the varied surroundings
of his position. The latter is the experience of the perfect, victorious Man who
lived in the true environment. He consciously lived, and moved, and had His
being in God, so that He could say, "I
am alone, yet not alone, for My Father is
with Me"; and in that environment He
was Master of every other—He put His
hand upon every opposing force, and
transmuted it by the power and magnificence of His pure manhood into an occasion of victory, into a stepping-stone
to the very throne of the universe. We
may go from that one notable illustration
to others from every age of the Christian
Church. Every true Christian is an illustration of this same great fact of men
and women moving out of the realm of
the false into the true, and becoming
victors over the very forces that hitherto

had damaged and debased them. Out
of circumstances that thwarted and hin-
dered, God has made His fairest saints.

III

Now, thirdly and lastly, let us look at
the inter-relation of these questions. Environment must have a basis on which
to work. Suppose, for the sake of argument, that there is in front of us a garden, well watered, carefully tilled, prop-
erly tended. The soil is rich and fertile.
I am going to bring into that garden
something that I may plant there; and I
hold in my hands two things: a pebble
that I have picked from the seashore—
smooth and beautiful in form—and an
acorn that has just been shaken from the
oak by autumn's blast. I suppose for
the moment that I do not know the nature of these two things. They are about
the same size; they are not unlike in appearance; there may be a difference in
their weight, but in most respects they
appear to the casual observer to be very
much alike. I put the pebble in the

garden; I put the acorn in the garden. The environment is the same in both cases, the soil is the same, and the same sun with shafts of light will penetrate the soil, and the same soft showers will reach the pebble and the acorn. But you have already solved my riddle, and this is no problem to you. The acorn will burst its shell in spring; and we pass rapidly over the intervening centuries, and there it stands, a proud oak battling against the blasts of winter, and in its turn shedding acorns on the ground. Where is the pebble? No one has disturbed its resting-place. It is there still, a lonely pebble. The environment is the same—what, then, is the difference? Environment must have a basis. In the pebble there was no germ of life; in the acorn there was. The perfect environment of soil and light and air upon the pebble produced no result; but upon the acorn it produced the springing of life out of death.

"In God we live, and move, and have our being"; and there is no exception.

It is not the preacher, the Church members, the Christian people merely, that in God do "live, and move, and have their being." Every soul—the most profligate man, the most licentious man, the most greedy man, the most ungodly man, "lives, and moves, and has his being in God." Life to one man means growth, advancement, movement ever on, until that man is as a tree planted by the rivers of water, and his influence is going out, not only in his own generation, but to the generation of generations. The other man, living in the same environment, is unmoved thereby. God Himself cannot act upon that man so as to produce the fruit, and life, and beauty that are being produced in an identical environment in the case of his brother man. Now, wherein lies the difference? In the one the spirit-life is dead. To use an expression of Scripture, so glibly quoted, and yet so little trembled at, that man is "dead in trespasses and sins." His lower life is there, the physical basis is there; but that never consciously touches

God. Flesh and blood cannot inherit
the Kingdom of God. The mental vigor
is still there—keen and wondrous; but
that never consciously touches God, for
"no man by searching can find out
God." The spirit neglected, starved, is
dead; and that man living in God never
feels Him, never responds to the tender,
gracious influences of the Divine heart
and the Divine strength. This man, on
the other hand, has spirit dominant, and
has recognized that man is more than
matter and mental power, and recog-
nizing it, has yielded himself to Divine
control, and in that act of yielding he
has been born again. He has passed
from death unto life; he has become a
new creature. For him "old things have
passed away and all things have become
new," so that he touches God and feels
the Eternal, and communes with the Divine; and that touch, that feeling, that
communion, are creating character, and
building it for the palace and the home
of the Eternal. One man lives in his
environment consciously, because his

own spirit is quickened by the Eternal Spirit of God. The other, living in the same environment, does not know it, because he is dead in his trespasses and in his sins.

In a few closing sentences I want to make a personal application of this study in order that I may help some soul who feels the contradiction and the difficulty of environment.

Man is saying: "Certainly I could be a Christian IF I could get out of this position; if I could get out of this business; this particular situation in which I am engaged, where there are ungodly men round about me. If I only lived in your home instead of mine, I could be a Christian. My environment is against me."

If you cannot be a Christian where you are, you cannot be a Christian anywhere. God is no more in my home than in thine.

"It is so easy to be Christians while we are in the sanctuary, and the very breath of eternity is upon us and God is at hand. To-morrow in the city, in the workshop, in the office, on the mart, it is very hard."

God is no more in the sanctuary than He is in your shop, or your office, or the mart; and it is no more difficult to pray when ungodly men are thronging around you than it is to pray here.

So long as you are longing for freedom from your present environment to be a Christian, you will never find the deliverance you seek.

What, then, is needed? That you should believe what you think you believe. The most difficult thing to get a man to believe is the thing which he thinks he does believe. You believe in God—you live, and move, and have your being in Him. Believe that—believe that only, believe that supremely, and then begin life in that belief. And in that belief, believe above everything else that

> "Hell is nigh, but God is nigher,
> Circling you with hosts of fire."

The poor trembling servant of the prophet, when he saw the "host with horses and chariots round about the

city," said, "Alas, my master! how shall
we do?" It was a false vision of environment. But the prophet had the true
vision. He replied: "Fear not; for
they that be with us are more than they
that be with them." Then he prayed,
"Lord, I pray Thee, open his eyes that
he may see." The servant looked, and
"behold, the mountain was full of horses
and chariots of fire round about Elisha."

That is the lesson. God is superior to
the slum or the tenement; to ungodly
companions or influence God is greater
than the sneer of the mocker. Live in
God consciously, and thou hast found
the environment that is highest and clos-
est and strongest, the environment which
is superior to all others.

Yes; but how can I get to God? "No
man cometh unto the Father but by Me."
"Come unto Me, all ye that are weary
and heavy laden, and I will give you
rest." "Him that cometh to Me I will
in no wise cast out."

May God help us to believe the things
we think we believe.

III

HEREDITY

"For as by one man's disobedience many were made sinners, so by the obedience of one shall many be made righteous. Moreover, the law entered, that the offence might abound. But where sin abounded, grace did much more abound: that as sin hath reigned unto death, even so might grace reign through righteousness unto eternal life by Jesus Christ our Lord."—ROMANS v. 19–21.

III

HEREDITY

THE subject as announced is that of Heredity; but I want to take another word, Inheritance, because it is a larger word in its application to these great truths. Heredity tells only half of the story of human inheritance. Something else must be told concerning every soul, and the telling of that something else is the telling of the provision of God's love.

Every babe is, as Charles Kingsley sang, "heir of all the ages gain"; and every child starts out upon the journey of life with certain inheritances, for which he has either to thank or curse his forerunners. Whether we go back to the old theological statement of this doctrine, and speak of the fall of man, and of the effect that fall has produced upon the whole human race right to this time, or no, we must all admit this truth.

It is being preached to us, both from the pulpit and the scientific platform, that man is connected with those who have gone before him so closely that he is influenced directly and positively by them. I am not attempting to explain the mystery of it—that is not my domain; I announce the fact.

This paragraph includes the whole problem; and in forceful, clear, intelligent language makes a statement concerning it to which we are bound to pay attention, because of its paramount importance. Our scheme is, firstly, to consider this subject of heredity as a part of human inheritance; secondly, to consider the apostle's statement concerning grace as complementary; and thirdly, to endeavor to deduce from that twofold consideration the possibilities which lie before every one of us, as we face life with all its mystery and its conflict.

I

In the first place, we shall consider the Biblical statement of the law of heredity.

"For as by one man's disobedience many were made sinners." There are hundreds of men to-day who put their hand upon that verse and quarrel with its theological statement, who, nevertheless, are preaching this great doctrine of heredity. Magazine writers tell us that what a man is, what a man does, and what a man will finally become, depend upon the color of his hair, upon the form of his physical being, upon what some one was before him. But if you tell them that doctrine is acknowledged, recognized here in the theology of Paul, those men are astonished; and yet it is so. "By one man's disobedience many were made sinners."

When life becomes something more to me than a game; when I cease to look upon the days as opportunities for play —and every man does sooner or later feel that life is more than a game, the world other than a mere playground— then I look out upon my future and hear the call of the Divine. Within the heart of the thinking man as he faces life, there sound voices calling him to high and noble living. He may not be able to understand or explain them; he may not detect from whence they come, or whose they are—those strange, luring voices— but they are there. Then that man awakens to find that he is not free from vices which he has not chosen; he realizes that there lies within the confines of his own individuality—in what realm he can hardly tell; whether physical, mental, or spiritual, he is hardly cognizant in those early days—a tendency that propels him, and inclinations that draw him along certain lines of life.

Let us understand that those inclinations and tendencies—the dominant inclinations and tendencies of that man's life—may not be evil. A man may find, some summer morning, when the king of day is just lighting the mountains with his coming glory, edging them with a golden hue, and the dew is quivering and sparkling upon the grass, and the voice of the bird is all that breaks the hushed stillness—he may find that within

him there dwells the sacred muse. He
was a born poet; but he never discovered it until that morning. How did it
happen? You cannot explain the mystery. You may philosophize concerning
it, and argue about it; but there it is.

It may be that he discovered—on some
evening when the sun went westering,
bathing the clouds with a wondrous
glory, tinging them with gold, and telling the weary watchers that behind the
darkness there was the very splendor of
God—that he was an artist; he was that
before, but he had not recognized it. He
had inherited it. It had come to him
after skipping—in some strange and un-
accountable fashion—one or more generations, bringing into his life the poetry
of those who had gone before; the
power to see, which some forerunner
had.

But almost more constantly man awakens to find that the thing within him—
which is there without his consent, without his creating—is an evil thing. He
awakes to find that a certain desire in

his life, which in itself is natural—and to
say that, using the word *natural* in its
true sense, is to say that it is pure—is
distorted and out of shape. He awakes
to find that there is a passionate desire,
making demands, and crying with force
and energy and unceasing earnestness,
"Give me, satisfy me; meet my need";
in other words, a man awakes to find
that lust, and passion, and greed, and
evil are in him. He looks out upon life,
heavily handicapped from the first, without a chance. Let us look these things
squarely in the face, for this is the true
story of many a man's life.

Take the most familiar illustrations
that you have dealt with yourself again
and again; the story of how a man
awakens to find that he was born a
drunkard, and another man awakens to
find that he was born impure. He cannot deny it. If the great crowd have
never realized these things, it is because
the fires of passion have not been in-
tense, because in their lives there has
been no consuming sense of this great

fact—but there it is. I talked to a man
some year or two ago who was drink-
ing. I shall never forget the way he ap-
palled me, as with passionate earnestness
he looked into my face and, said, "Sir,
don't talk to me about drink." "But
why?" I asked. "Because," he said,
"you are ignorant concerning it." "But
what do you mean?" "You talk to me
about a desire for it, and you know nothing of what you are talking about. Do
you know that my father and his father
both committed suicide while in delirium
tremens? Drink!" he said; "you put a
glass of wine there, and tell me of a certainty, upon the oath of God, that if I
drink I will be shot—I would drink it!"

We have to face these facts. Young
men who are going from our city and
country homes are suddenly over-
whelmed, and fall in the conflict. Why?
They did not choose the sinful things;
but suddenly, under certain conditions
of life, they find a devil in them that had
been sleeping. Somehow he is aroused,
and he masters them. They have inher-

ited evil tendencies from some one gone before. So that I say to-day men are starting in life from this standpoint without the semblance of a chance; they are handicapped in the race from the beginning, and from before their birth.

That is exactly what the apostle says here: "By one man's disobedience"—and whether that man be Adam or your father, it does not affect the matter—"By one man's disobedience many were made sinners." That is the great law: sinners by birth; sinners by the very force that dwells within them, and for which they are not responsible. Such is the story of the lives of thousands of our fellow-men to-day. What have we to say to these things? What has the preacher to say? What has the Church of Jesus Christ to say? What has the gospel of Jesus Christ to say?

II

It has to say that there is another truth which Jesus Christ came to proclaim, side by side with that first one; and that

the man who only declares that, tells but
half the common truth of every life and
soul of man. And what is the other
truth ? It is contained in this same passage to the Romans, and the 20th verse,
" Where sin abounded, grace did much
more abound"; and that statement of the
20th verse is linked to the second half of
the 19th verse: " So by the obedience of
one shall many be made righteous.
Where sin abounded grace did much
more abound."

In order that we may understand the
force of this gospel of the grace of God
—and this really is the gospel of the grace
of God—we must get back from that
position upon which we have been
standing, and consider it from a different
standpoint. First of all we must come
to understand that God always deals
with man personally and individually.
This seems a very difficult statement in
face of what we have been saying.

Those of you who have read Ezekiel
xviii., will remember that it opens with
a challenge on the part of God to the

people of Israel, and the challenge is
this: "How say ye, The fathers have
eaten sour grapes, and the children's
teeth are set on edge?" That proverb
has not dropped out of use; men are
perpetually using it. You will hear it
in conversation to-day and to-morrow.
You will hear the story of some young
man's wrongdoing, and hear some one
commenting upon it; and of the wrongdoing of his father, saying, with a wise
look and a shake of the head, that has
more in it than all the speech: "Yes, the
fathers have eaten sour grapes, and the
children's teeth are set on edge."
"Well, but," you say, "is it not true?"
Absolutely untrue. That proverb that is
binding and misleading men is absolutely false. There is no truth in it.
"Surely, but it is in the Bible?" Twice.
It is both in Ezekiel and Jeremiah. But
it is there in order that it may be contra-
dicted. You search the context out for
yourselves. It is not a clear, lucid, true,
correct statement of God's dealing with
men to say, "The fathers eat, and the

children's teeth are set on edge." God does not punish a son for his father's wrongdoing. "Oh, but surely that is not correct. Do we not read in Exodus, where the law is given, 'I the Lord thy God am a jealous God, visiting the iniquities of the fathers upon the children even unto the third and fourth generation.' Does it not say that?" No. "Oh, but it does." Find it and read it. I will let any man read it who can find it. It does not say it at all; it is not in the Book, my friend. "Then, what does it say?" Listen, "I the Lord thy God am a jealous God, visiting the iniquities of the fathers upon the children unto the third and fourth generation *of them that hate Me.*" And you have no right to miss out these five words, and rob the whole passage of its essential meaning. What is its essential meaning? If the generations continue to hate, they will have punishment; and it goes still further—"and showing mercy unto thousands of them that love Me." And that is what Ezekiel says. God says: "All souls are Mine; I take man by man, individually"; and if the father is a good man and the son is evil, the son shall be punished; and if the father is an evil man, and the son is righteous, the son is not to be punished for the evil of the father, but he is to live.

But is not this more difficult of comprehension; for remember, I emphasize it and abide by it. I want you to see that God does not visit the iniquity of the father upon the children; that God does not smite, and strike, and burn a man, even in this life, because his father was evil. Why, the whole conception is blasphemy.

Then what are we to do? We are side by side and face to face with two apparently contradictory statements. Man does not start fair in life; he is handicapped through hereditary tendencies in his blood. If he sin, he is punished; and yet you tell me that God takes man by himself, and deals with him without reference to what his father was. Perfectly true. I am not going to call into question the character of God, to lay this down as something I am bound to discover somewhere or other, in some way or other. If this law be a law of life from which I cannot escape, that I inherit the tendencies to wrong from my father; and if it be also law that God takes me, and deals with me, and punishes or rewards me, without any reference to my connection with my father, then in order to do that, He must, somewhere and somehow, provide an antidote to the poison which is already in my veins. He must bring to me, side by side with the tendencies to wrong, something that shall be at any rate as strong as that tendency, and that is able to overcome it. That is the logical statement of the thing as I understand it; that is, if God be "just"—I will not say "love." I want to put this superlatively, especially to some young man feeling the force of some hereditary taint, and help him, as the gospel has helped me.

I have a tendency to a form of evil in

my nature and in my blood; and then I
come here and I read, "God will not
punish my father if I go wrong. The
soul that sinneth, IT shall die." And I
take my stand in one of those solemn
moments of life to which man comes
when he rises in his true dignity, and,
realizing he has a right to deal with God,
he says, in the presence of the Holy
One, "I did not choose to be born with
this tendency to evil. It is here without
my choice and without my consent; and
if Thou, O God, art going to deal with
me upon the pure line of righteousness,
without reference to the things I have received from my forefathers, then, if
Thou art a just God, Thou must provide
an antidote of force greater than the
force that is born within me, that will
quench its fires and set me free; and I
am bold to say, if the gospel has no message like that, it is no gospel for me."
It may be a gospel for a man who has
not experienced the fires of passion.
From a gospel that merely says, "Copy
this perfect example," I turn away; for

it cannot be mine because of the fires that exhaust my physical power, dethrone my mental vigor, paralyze my brain, and dim my vision. I must have a negation of evil, stronger than the negation of good that flows in my veins, and throbs in my nerves, and masters me, whether I will or not. Now, that much I say, God must do what my text tells me He has done. Just as " by one man's sins or disobedience, many were made sinners, so by the obedience of one shall many be made righteous."

What is this story, then ? It is the old story that I need not stay to tell. It is the story of the coming from heaven of God to tabernacle in human flesh, and live human life, and meet human temptation, and overcome all that temptation. It is the story of God suffering for sin; it is the story of the Cross upon which the pure life of the one perfect Man was given as a ransom for many, so that by His coming, and His pure living, and His sacrificial dying, He has brought to every soul a second inheritance, the inheritance

of powerful, forceful, valuable righteousness.

Am I born to passion's fires? I am
also born to the quenching power of the
love of Jesus. Am I born with tendencies to wrong? I am also born to that
Holy Spirit as a birthright which can
hold, keep, and purify me, and present
me at last in the very presence of God.
Do you tell me to-night that your father,
or his father, or some one generations
back, was given over to some fearful
form of sin, and that, although it has
been slumbering for two generations, it
has reappeared in your life; and do you
tell me, with a wail of anguish, that that
is your inheritance—that awful form of
sin, that has gripped you with irresisti-
ble tenacity, and thwarted you at every
turn? My brother, I tell you that there
is another inheritance; that you are born
to the life of Christ. When you come
here, the story is so old that men have
begun to be uninterested. Oh, how one
longs, not for a new theology, but for a
new setting and phrasing of it, that shall

arrest the thought of men to-day! I am not here to preach morality as a beautiful thing—every one believes it. We are all agreed upon that. I do not think there is anybody, I do not care how far down he may be, who does not believe that purity, and righteousness, and morality, are lovely attributes of man's nature. I am not here to talk about that, I announce this fact: that where there is a man fast bound with chains of sin and passion and lust, Christ by the power of His Holy Spirit can shatter those chains, and quench those fires, and set that man free.

You, my brother, have a twofold inheritance: you have the inheritance to evil which has mastered you hitherto, and thwarted your best intentions; and you have also the inheritance in the power of Jesus Christ that is to come in, and be the force that releases you.

Oh, accept it, will you, not as theory, but as fact proven again and again in the past nineteen hundred years; proven again and again in this very year. If we could only institute a strict enquiry, there are thousands of souls who would testify to this fact: "I was the slave of sin, of lust, of passion, of greed, of unrighteousness; but Jesus Christ coming into my life by the power of the Holy Spirit, has set me free." And when they have borne their testimony, we will be hard and critical, and say, "That is the testimony of thy own lips; so now tell me what do thy neighbors and friends say? Let the worldly man come in and tell me how that man lives who is a Christian, and the testimony from the world will be overwhelming." "We have seen the transformation wrought by the Son of God; we have seen our neighbors—irascible, sour, hard-hearted—become tender, sweet, loving, compassionate, like the very Son of God Himself." The testimony is on every hand. Have we not a right to apply a scientific test to that matter, as to all others? If we can find one man, a thousand men, a million men, in the course of the ages of the Christian era, who have been absolutely transformed, perfectly re-made, changed, so that there was no comparison between what they are and what they were, have we not a right to say something has wrought this ? And have we not a right to accept that great united testimony as it comes upon us—that what has wrought it has been the grace of God ?

My brother, I want you to see the force of this. It is not merely that there is for you an inheritance of a power to be righteous which is equivalent to the power of evil. I like the grandeur and the overwhelming magnificence of Paul's expression, "Where sin abounded, grace did much more abound." What are the possibilities that grow out of it ? Let us simply put our hands on them. That is all we can do. "That," in the last verse, "as sin hath reigned, grace may reign through righteousness unto eternal life." There are three points, then, of the result of the coming into this life of the power of the grace of Jesus Christ. The three points are these: (1) Regnant sin is deposed, and (2) in its place the grace of Jesus Christ takes the throne and reigns;

and (3) the result is "eternal life"; and
that eternal life is not merely life that is
long-continued, but life that is broad and
wide and magnificent in its possibilities.

III

Now, to gather up the great lessons
that I want to inscribe upon your hearts
and mine.   You have inherited a tendency to evil.   I grant it you. You didn't
choose it. You were born with it. Now
listen: God never yet has, and never will,
punish any man for inheriting anything.

In the next place, let me say that heredity is not the final word.   Reverting to
what I said at the commencement—the
color of your hair, and the shape of
your head, and your temperament, are
not all the story of your own life. What
is the other side ? The grace of God; the
Spirit of God. Grace is the complement;
grace is the negative of sin. You are
born with a tendency to sin, but you are
also born into the birthright of the life
and passion of the Son of God; and so
Jesus Christ becomes the touchstone of

character. Reject Him, and you are a
victim to those tendencies which are
slumbering within your own nature; but
accept Him, and you may put your conquering foot upon every enemy that faces
you, and in His name have the victory.

Thus Christ becomes the touchstone of
judgment. The question before the throne
of eternal righteousness will be, "What
did this man and that man do with Jesus?"
It will not be available for me to say in the
day of that final judgment, "O God, I
was born with a tendency to the sin that
ruined me: is there no excuse for me?"
for the answer of the impartial Judge
would be, "If thou wast born with a
tendency to sin, thou wast also born into
the birthright of the conquering life of
Jesus Christ, and thou didst deliberately
choose to reject the life and cling to the
death; then that choice seals thy doom"·
and so, by this provision of grace, every
man still stands alone in his responsibility to God. Every man has this chance
—the chance of what Jesus did for him
upon the Cross of His passion. The

whole truth concerning my inheritance is not told until I have understood that it is a twofold inheritance, from Adam and from Jesus Christ.   With this difference, that my inheritance from those who have gone before me comes to me along the line of succession; but my inheritance in Jesus Christ He has trusted to no line of succession, but He brings it to me Himself, by the power of His Spirit, and deals with me in direct personal communion.

Dost thou feel that passion fires are slumbering within thee ?   Give thyself to the Son of God; and by His Holy Spirit He will quench the fires, and hold you in the hollow of His own pierced hand, and make you pure as He Himself is pure, in the day that He presents you to His Father. All tendency to sin may be overcome, and is overcome when souls are surrendered to the Christ of God.

IV

SPIRITUAL ANTAGONISM

"Then was Jesus led up of the Spirit into the wilderness to be tempted of the devil."—MATT. iv. 1.

"For in that He Himself hath suffered being tempted, He is able to succor them that are tempted." —HEB. ii. 18.

IV

SPIRITUAL ANTAGONISM

PERHAPS one of the greatest and most mysterious problems of life is that of spiritual antagonism. Beyond the disabilities of environment and heredity there is yet this other. To every soul there comes from without an intelligent suggestion of evil, enticement toward evil, provision for evil.

Quite apart from the temptations which come to us from the ordinary environment of everyday living, or from the tendencies toward evil with which we are born, there is this subtlest, profoundest danger; in other words, we have to contend not only with the world and the flesh, but also with the devil.

There are great mysteries concerning the existence of these spiritual adversaries which I do not stay to discuss.

Let it only be said, here and now, that to
my own heart one of the great sources
of hope, in life and work and outlook, is
to be found in the supreme conviction
that I hold of the existence of actual
spiritual enemies. Did I not believe in
the existence of Satan and his emissaries,
then I must believe that all the dark and
dreadful deeds that smirch the page of
human history have their origin in human
nature. This I do not believe. Outside
our planet there is evil, sin, wrong; these
are not the natural products of that great
creation of God, of which we form not
only a part, but the crown and glory:
evil is not indigenous to the soil of the
earth, it is an importation; and its existence in other realms is a mystery, absolutely beyond the possibility of our ex-
plaining or understanding.

We have to face the fact of its existence, side by side with that other sublimer
fact, that our aspirations are Godward.
We have endeavored, so far, to think of
the evil that is around and within; now
we consider these spiritual antagonisms,

and desire to learn how we are to combat these forces, so as to gain complete victory over them.

Jesus came to reveal God to man. He came also to reveal man to man. Apart from Him—His person, His character, His teaching—we can have no true conception of the Divine ideal for man; but in Him we have a concrete example of the great thought that possessed the mind of Deity when God said, "Let us make man."

May I take you one step further upon the line of the truth that Jesus is the Revealer, and say that He came not only to reveal God and Man, but also those very spiritual forces that oppose us? It is only as we study the life and conflict of the perfect Man that we are able to understand all the subtlety and the power of the enemies that are against us. Out of obscurity into brightest light He dragged these forces; and from His dealing with them we are to learn our relationship to them, and the possibility of our triumph over them. Man had been tempted and

tried in all the ages. Prior to His coming, these forces had ever been busy
spoiling the work of God and marring
its beauty. He came and revealed the
enemies in the light of His pure life. No
part of that revelation of Satan is more
startling, more vivid, more commanding,
than the story to which this first verse of
Matthew iv. is the introduction.

He went, the last Adam, no longer to
the perfect environment of the Garden of
Eden, but to the loneliness and the deadly
desolation of the wilderness, in order
that His humanity might pass beyond the
stage of innocence into that of holiness;
that He might not only be innocent and
pure, but triumphant over the forces of
evil that had wrecked all before. Satan
confronted Him with threefold temptation—to make stones into bread; to se-
cure the kingdoms of the world; to fling
Himself from the pinnacle of the temple.
With that story, so familiar to us all, as
a background, we shall proceed to consider, firstly, the *revelation of evil* that
Jesus gives; secondly, *His conquest of*

evil: and from that twofold consideration we shall draw the comfort of the
second verse that I have chosen, "That
He Himself having suffered being
tempted, is able to succor them that are
tempted."

I

What, then, is the revelation of evil
that we have in this wilderness scene?

(1)   That evil as represented by Satan
in his attack upon the Christ is audacious
effrontery. The devil is impulsed by
everything foreign to the nature of God.
"God is Love"; but Satan is the embodi-
ment of cruel hate. "God is Light";
but Satan's suggestions are of the very
nature of darkness. "God is Liberty";
but if you scrutinize these temptations,
you will find that they are designed to
enslave.

Jesus is the realization of all the will
and purpose of the Father. "God is
Love"; at once He is the tenderest and
strongest expression of that love. "God
is Light"; He is the most perfect out-

shining of that light.   " God is Liberty ";
He is the Son, making men free indeed.
Through all the years of His life, prior to
this hour of temptation, He has lived in
the fierce light of the Eternal Throne of
purity and righteousness, and no single
flaw has there been in His obedience.

Yet such is the insolence of hell, that
it will attempt to blight even such beauty.
We learn, therefore, that no regard for
conduct will prevent his approach; no
purity of yesterday will be sufficient to
hinder him from attempting to render the
soul impure.

(2) In the second place, we have a
revelation of the *subtlety* of evil.   Evil
chooses its time of attack.   There is no
moment when the soul of man is more
susceptible to the onslaught of evil than
after some high vision and ecstasy.   Jesus
had come from the seclusion of Nazareth
to the waters of His baptism, where He
had heard the voice of the Father saying,
"This is My beloved Son, in Whom I
am well pleased."

The moment when we are most in

danger of attack is the moment immediately following some new vision of God. The devil chooses his time.

The subtlety is more clearly evinced, however, in the fact that he advances upon legal lines. A hungry man must provide bread for himself. "If Thou be the Son of God," says the tempter, "command these stones that they be made bread." That is the first temptation; satisfaction for physical need—not a desire for luxury, but necessity—bread. He does not come to the pure Soul in the awful loneliness of the wilderness with a temptation to evil in some repulsive form, but with a suggestion that He should provide something that is right in itself. Make for Thyself bread, O hungry Man; tired and weary with the waiting and loneliness of forty days—bread!

Not only does he advance upon legal lines, but he bases his temptation upon the very highest relationships. "If Thou be the Son of God"—he does not say, "Yield Thy Sonship, set it aside"; but use it, and use it not for what appears to be wrong, but for that which is a natural demand—make bread. "If Thou wilt fall down and worship me, all these kingdoms, which in panoramic view I have stretched before Thy vision, shall be Thine." Here, also, he appeals to something which is right. It is to possess these kingdoms that this Man has come; it is to hold the sceptre of government over these kingdoms that He has lived, moved, and had His being among men. Satan only offers Him that which is right, when he suggests to Him that He should take the kingdoms.

Again, you will notice that he proceeds along the line of righteousness. He takes Him to the high mountain—the Soul in loneliness—and shows Him the kingdoms of the earth, and suggests, not that He should give up fealty and worship, but that He *shall* worship, and that He shall worship one who appears to have a right over these kingdoms.

Once more he brings Him to a high pinnacle of the temple, and says, "If Thou be the Son of God, cast Thyself

down; for it is written, 'He shall give
His angels charge concerning Thee; and
in their hands they shall bear Thee up,
lest at any time Thou dash Thy foot
against a stone.'" What can be more
beautiful in a beautiful soul, more pure
in a pure soul, more saintly in a saint,
than that the beautiful, pure, saintly One
should abandon Himself to the strength
and tenderness of the Father? "Here
is an opportunity for Thee to prove the
Fatherhood of Thy Father, the tenderness of His love, the strength of His arm.
Step out upon Him, cast Thyself down,
go out of the common ruts in which
men so long have travelled in their trust,
or in their failure, and, by a magnificent
renunciation of Thy life, test thy Father's
love."

No, these temptations are not coarse,
low, vulgar, in the common acceptation
of those words; they are high, spiritual,
subtle, insidious, far-reaching temptations. Their meaning and force can only
be learned as we consider the resistance
of Christ to every one of them. We

need to know the subtlety of the foe
with whom we have to deal.

(3) Then, again, mark his *persistence.*
The conflict does not begin in the wilderness. For thirty years this Man has
faced temptation in some form or other.
Every day there has come against that
pure Soul some force of evil, and back-
ward each has been driven, unable to
storm the impenetrable barrier of Christ's
mighty purity. In every case He has put
the conquering foot of His humanity
upon the neck of His enemies, scattering
irretrievable ruin in their camp; and yet
Satan will come again, even though He
is now anew baptized with the Spirit
from on high. With strange and awful
persistence he will dog His footsteps to
the last. After that temptation, we read,
"The devil left Him for a little season."
Do you know when he finally left Him?
He left Him on the Resurrection morning, and never till then. He followed
Him to Gethsemane; and I hear the echo
of his temptation in the prayer of the
Christ, "If it be possible let this cup pass

from Me." He followed Him to the Cross; and the presence of this relentless, uncompromising, persistent foe is to be detected in that agonized prayer of the Son of God: "My God, My God, why hast Thou forsaken Me?" Never—until back from Hades and the shades of black darkness the conquering Man came, holding in His own pierced right hand the keys of darkness and death—did these forces leave Him or cease their attempts to conquer and spoil the life of the Son of God.

(4) But I have another word to say about evil as revealed in that temptation. Not only do I find its effrontery, subtlety, and persistence, but its *folly*. See the folly of evil when compared with righteousness. Mark how Satan, subtle beyond our comprehension, has only three avenues of attack; for, remember, these are typical, and no soul in the history of the world has ever been tempted except along one of these—Bread, Office, Trust. That is the threefold attack of the devil from the first to the last. Physical,

mental, spiritual. He has never yet understood the omnipotence of a soul "homed" in God. That pure white Soul in the wilderness cannot be beaten so long as He abides in God. Satan himself has not measured the depth, the infinity, the boundless spaces of the Most High, or he never would have commenced the struggle between his own comparative weakness, and the almightiness of God and righteousness.

Then we are to remember that these forces that are coming against us are characterized by their marvellous effrontery. When you feel you are safest from the attack of Satan, you are most in danger of becoming a victim to his wiles. Show me the man who has had some spiritual experience—call it conversion or second blessing, or anything you please—and who, coming out of that experience, says, "Now am I safe. I have passed the region of temptation; I have gained the mastery": and I show you the man in supremest danger. It is the man who clings tenaciously, out of the agonized sense of his own weakness, who is strong; and not the man who stands erect, and says temptation can have no power on him. Satan has no respect for any building, or convention, or religious frame of mind man has ever possessed. The pure soul of Jesus was met with temptation when the Divine voice had been heard, and the Divine approval declared.

Remember also, that these foes are subtle beyond all our knowing. Oh, we are so sure the devil cannot overcome us in certain ways; and we are quite right. Here is one man standing up in the great consciousness of his strength, and being very angry with the man who has failed. The man who never felt the fire and thirst for drink moving in his veins, pronounces his small anathema upon the drunkard in his cups, and says that Satan cannot tempt him like that. And he will never try! He is not such a fool! But he has tempted thee, and thou art falling—falling of pride and self-sufficiency, as thou dost dare to pass thy sentences upon thy fallen brother. Do not forget, the devil will not attack thee upon the place where thou art strongest. He will come where the door is weakest in its fastenings, and smite the chain on the link where the flaw is hidden.

Remember this, too: his temptations are always based upon that which is right. I believe if young men only learned that secret of temptation, it would be a great help to them. He suggests that you should do something. Now, everything is primarily right. It is perfectly right to have bread; to get the governments; and to trust God.

As to his persistency. Dear child of God, hast thou been following for forty, or even fifty, years in His footsteps? Thou art not safe. The devil will still dog your pathway. Upon the very approach to the pearly gates he will suggest a lie and a blasphemy.

Remember also his folly; but that will be more clearly seen as we think for a moment how the conquest of evil is revealed in this same story.

II

How was it that this Man conquered?
And the answer can be given in a very
few sentences. It is the simplicity of
the method that is its grandeur and its
strength. First of all, Jesus conquered
because, as the prophet Isaiah said of
Him, "He was keen of scent in the fear
of the Lord." He recognized a temptation to evil when He was asked to make
bread. He was asked to satisfy a right
craving in a wrong way. God had led
Him by the Spirit into the wilderness
to fast. To feed when God said fast,
was to sin. This may appear a matter
of small moment, but it is the basis of
all evil. There is no essential evil. Evil
is forevermore a prostitution of right.
Evil is an abuse of a good gift. Bread?
Certainly; but if God has said fast, then
there must be no bread, even though
death come on apace.

It was in the attempt to draw Him
from the will of God that the temptation
was centred; and Jesus, "keen of scent in
the fear of the Lord," detected, by reason

of His habitual communion with God, by reason of the Divine atmosphere in which He lived and moved and had His being— the evil that those not living so might have missed. My brother, if you are to overcome, you must live with God, and must become "keen of scent in the fear of the Lord." How often people have said to me, and I dare say you have heard it also, "But I was tempted, and I fell before I knew it." Quite true. It has been the story of many a sin in my own life. I was in the mire before I knew it. I ought to have known it. Had I been living in God, and depending on God when the slightest breath of evil came, I should have detected it. "To be forewarned is to be forearmed." To be conscious of your enemy is to be halfway to being victorious over him. Jesus lived in the Divine, and detected the evil.

Again, He had one refuge from all attacks; and that refuge was the Divine will. Whatever the attack, He remained there. He dwelt within the stronghold of the Divine government; and within that stronghold no force was able to overcome Him; and no attack, however violent, could shake the foundations of eternal righteousness and eternal justice, as evidenced in the will of God. "Command these stones that they be made bread." "It is written, 'Man shall not live by bread alone, but by every Word that proceedeth out of the mouth of God.'" "My life is not the life you think it is. O Satan; you imagine My life is physical, and needs bread. That is the probationary basis upon which life is being created and fashioned. Man does not live by bread alone": and so He abode in the will of God, refusing every alluring call. Staying there, He became more than Conqueror over the forces that assailed Him.

III

Now the gospel message for us is that of Hebrews. "He has suffered being tempted, and now He is able to succor." How can He succor? I can only answer this in sentences. Given the soul that yields to Him, what are the methods by which He succors that soul in the hour of temptation? First, He cleanses the nature; secondly, He restores that soul to its true environment, and makes it conscious of God; and then—oh, let me put it simply, I do not want any one to miss this, as the supreme thought of this study—then He, by His Spirit, takes up His abode within, and fights the battle and gets the victory. When the enemy comes in like a flood, He lifts up His standard against him. And so, when I am victorious over the assaults of spiritual antagonism, it is not because I am strong, but because I have given the key of the citadel into the hands of the thorn-crowned King, and He locks the door and Himself holds it; and when the enemy seeking spiritual devastation comes against me to assault my soul, and blight my life, and mar my character, it is not I that live, but Christ that liveth in me; and He repeats the conquest of the wilderness, and scatters my foes like chaff before the wind.

Thy secret place of victory, O my soul, is not the place where thou shalt assert thy strength; it is the place where thou shalt assert the strength of thy Master, and put Him as thy shield for evermore to quench the fiery darts of the evil one, and make Him the Captain of thy salvation to strike thy blow for thee, and get for thee thy victory. The whole story of victory over spiritual antagonism is clearly put in these words: "Submit thyself unto God; resist the devil, and he will flee from thee."

V

INFLUENCE

" For as by one man's disobedience many were made sinners, so by the obedience of One shall many be made righteous."—Rom. v. 19.

V

INFLUENCE

WE now proceed to consider the facts of heredity and environment from another standpoint; no longer as they affect us, but as through us they affect others. "No man liveth unto himself." Lonely, isolated life is an absolute impossibility by the very nature of man— an impossibility which has been proven in every successive generation, in all lands, and among all peoples. The life of every man is affecting, as well as being affected by, other persons. We desire to acquaint ourselves with the true Christian position in regard to this subject of our influence.

We shall firstly then state the case; secondly, examine it; and thirdly, consider solemnly the responsibilities entailed upon every one of us.

I

"As by one man's disobedience many were made sinners, so by the obedience of One shall many be made righteous." The simple statement of the text is that man is a centre and source of influence. The federal heads of the human race—the representative men through all the ages—are held up to our view, not only that the apostle may make a great theological statement; but in order that we may see them to be what they really are —each of them typical men.

The statement is not merely a declaration that we have inherited from Adam tendencies to sin, and from Christ redemptive forces. It is that, but it is much more: namely, an announcement that the positions they occupied were typical and representative of the position that every man, woman, and child occupies also. By disobedience the first man wrought havoc amid those that followed him. By obedience the second has produced the wondrous results which have made the desert blossom as the rose, and rivers of water to spring in dry and solitary places.

The influence, in each case, was determined by the life. Disobedience begat disobedience; obedience was the generating force of obedience. From the breaking of law arose not only sin in the individual case, but in the influence exercised; and, therefore, in succeeding generations. From the keeping of law comes the righteousness which has restored man to communion with God. This is true, not only in the one supreme example of the life of the Christ, but in all the men who have heard His voice, and been obedient to Him.

Every man is a new starting-point for good or for bad in the history of the human race. I am the heir of all the ages past. I am also a starting-point for ages to come. I have inherited forces without having been consulted. I shall also transmit to other ages by the effect of my life to-day, and by the influence that I am exerting upon those who touch me at every point, forces which will either make or mar the human race; which will be for the uplifting or degradation of untold thousands of my kind. It is a principle of which one must speak in the first person singular, in order to lead thought in the line of individual application.

It is not for me merely to declare a theory, but for us to isolate ourselves; and, in the presence of God to face this fact, "No man liveth unto himself." Every one of us exerts influences which will have their effect upon other lives, and the generations yet unborn will be lifted nearer God or thrust into deeper darkness, because we have lived and moved and had our being on this earth.

II

So far we have stated the philosophy of the subject. Let us now make application of the same to our everyday life. We spoke of heredity so far as it affects us. Let us now remember that we, too, are transmitting forces, tendencies, biases, to those who come after us. Your disposition—whatever that may be, you know; your supreme tendencies—whatever they are, you know also; your character—all these influences are being repeated by the very fact of your life.

Human life is for evermore going out and touching other human life, taking hold of it, moulding it, and repeating itself upon it. Two men cannot live together in close companionship for many years without each becoming somewhat what the other is. True that the stronger will impress itself more deeply on the weaker; but the stronger will partake something of the weaker likewise.

It is a common everyday truth which has, perhaps, its supreme illustration in the consideration of child-life. How often we are driven, if we preach the gospel of Jesus Christ, to get among the children for the learning of our lessons. It becomes necessary that we do as the Master did by the seashore—call the child, who plays amid the pebbles, and put it into the midst of the disciples, that they may learn the lessons of the Kingdom. It is impossible for any man, whatever his position in the realm of thought may be, to deny that men bequeath to their children their dispositions, their tendencies, their character. We agree that we have received these things from those that have gone before us. In common honesty, and by a logical sequence, from which there can be no possible escape, we must also agree that we are transmitting them to those who are following us.

Not only is it true of heredity, but also of environment. You communicate your ideal to your friend; and the man who works with you, and hears your conversation, and watches your habits of life, will take from you your estimate of human life, and of the hereafter. All the history of social life witnesses to this.

But all this is so commonplace and ordinary. We have heard it so many times before; we were warned by our fathers and mothers, and told in the Sabbath-school class, and have heard it from preachers incessantly, that we have an influence. But may we not thrust this closer home, and say there is one inexorable law that men have not believed, although they have heard it perpetually—of the effect of influence—and that inexorable law may be written off in this form: *I am only able to exert the influence of my true self.* How many a man imagines he can influence his neighbor by what he says to him! He cannot. How many a man dreams he can influence children by the precepts that fall from his lips! Child-life is never so influenced. One step further. How many a man imagines he can influence his children, friends, neighbors, acquaintances, by what he desires they should think him to be! No man does so influence any of his fellows. How many a man, for many long years, has kept up an outward appearance of morality and respectability yea, even of religion, while his heart has not been cleansed; and in the deep recesses of his nature there have lurked, dominating all the impulses of that life, things low, and base, and impure! Tell

me, how has that man influenced other
men ? Has he influenced them by what
he has appeared to be, or by what he has
really been ? Without a moment's hesitation, I assert he has influenced men by
what he has been within himself. Not
by the appearance which was a lie, but
by the baseness which was the truth of
his life has he influenced children, and
friends, and acquaintances.

You may take that truth and turn it in
another form, if you will; and I know
this other side is a more startling thing
to orthodox believers than the first.
Here is a man who tells me he is not
a Christian; but who, when the King
begins to analyze these little words of
human speech—that have never given
utterance to the deep things of human
life—will be found to have meant, "*I
am not what Christianity has too often
seemed to be, a contradiction of Jesus
Christ.*" But that man by sweetness of
life, pureness of thought, and upright-
ness of living, has been exerting an influence upon others; and in the name of

the influence he has exerted, notwith-
standing the denial of his lips, I claim
him as one of Christ's men.

When we reach the Judgment-seat of
Jesus Christ, we shall have a great many
startling surprises; and what one of the
"old fathers" said will be true again and
again. "Methinks I shall see three won-
ders developed—and the first wonder
will be that I have ever reached its shining shore; the second, that I shall miss
large numbers that I thought were going
there; and the third will be that I shall
meet large numbers that I never thought
to see there." Do not let us forget that.
Christ came to create—not a creed, not a
formula of doctrine, not a profession in
orthodoxy which may become the most
veritable heterodoxy, but—character.
Oh that we could write that in letters of
living flame across the sky, that all men
might see it! What a man is, is the one
question with God; and if through the
bungling mistakes of so-called Christen-
dom pure souls have been driven from
our Shibboleths; if they have found

righteousness all unknowingly through Jesus Christ, and have exerted an influence that has drawn men to God—I claim them as Christ's own men by the influence they have exerted.

Does not the Master give His positive sanction to influence as a supreme test, when He says, "He that is not with Me is against Me; and he that gathereth not with Me scattereth abroad." Did He not mean to say, "If a man gathers with Me, he is with Me"; even though, perchance, the disciples said, "We had better destroy him with our fire, because he followeth not with us"; and the Master rebuked them, and said, "Ye know not what manner of spirit ye are of."

If a man is base, and impure, and sordid, and evil in himself, then all his church-membership and all his profession is as nothing. Men will be moved, not by what a man says, nor by what a man says he is, but by what he actually is. I claim that this is an inexorable law of influence—that a man exerts upon other people the influence of what he is, and not the influence of what he says, or even of what he says he is.

We must all exert influence, whether we will or no. You cannot shut yourself up from other men unless you actually betake yourself away from them. It is impossible, in this age, with humanity so inter-related as it is. Take the simplest illustration, and think of how many men you have to do with on any given day: think of the men who call at your door and leave the necessities of life for you; and the men who come to your office to see you on business; and the men of whom you ask your way in the street; and the man who drives you: and remember you never touch a man without influencing him.

F. B. Meyer has said, that the extra sixpence to the cabman has done more for Christianity than his preaching on many occasions. Think it out. You influence every man you touch by the way you look at him, and speak to him; and all the time the influence you are exerting is welling up out of your actual self, and you cannot prevent it. If thou knowest that thou art impure, know this also, that thy impurity is contagious. Thou canst not conceal in thy breast impurity and say, "I will be impure here, and not influence others." It spreads like the contagion of a fever, unknown as to the moments of its going, but deadly in the effects it produces.

III

What, then, is the duty that this great truth of influence entails upon every one of us? Does it not contain a rousing call to self-examination? Perfect collectivism can only grow out of the perfecting of individualism. You never can have a society organized to perfection. It must grow to perfection through the growth of the individuals that form it.

If that be true—and who will deny it?—then collectivism, society at large, has a right to make distinct and forceful demands upon every single individual. Society has a right to say to every soul, "Soul, for our sake, for the sake of the larger whole, be pure and strong." No man has a right to say he is master of himself, that he may please himself. The larger law, the more binding law, is that law that demands purity from the individual, for the sake of society. To exert a destructive influence is the most terrible sin that is possible to any man. No man has any right to perpetuate evil. If the influence of your life is an impure one, by the necessity of your own character, one of two things you should certainly do. You should either go to the great source of purification, or take yourself away from home, and friends, and society, and live out all the remainder of your impure days in the desert place, in order that the foul influence of your soul may not contaminate other men. "No man liveth unto himself"—let me repeat the solemn words— and society has a right with myriad-tongued voice to call on thee, "O soul of man, be pure and strong and true, not merely for thy own sake, but for the sake of the world."

My influence is tested by my relationship to this text. I shall exert a pure,
strong influence upon my fellow-men, if
I am an obedient soul. I shall exert an
impure influence upon them, notwith-
standing all other influences, if I am a
disobedient soul. What I want to press
upon your attention, and your thought,
is—your responsibility in this matter.
Men do not come to Jesus Christ—as
witness the whole history of the preaching of His Cross,—until they feel deep
in their own spirit the need of His wondrous work. It was not idly spoken in
the early days that repentance toward
God should come before faith toward
our Lord Jesus Christ. Nor was it idly
spoken hundreds of years before the
Master came, when the prophet, address-
ing the people of his time, said, "Let the
wicked forsake his way, and the unrighteous man his thoughts, and let him
return unto the Lord."

Until men have seen their own individual helplessness, there will be no
coming to the rivers of cleansing and the

life of Christ for the power that is necessary for pure, strong living. Therefore, I charge upon you again, in conclusion, this solemn warning—not only that you are exerting an influence, but that you are responsible for that influence. Oh, my brother, if you have an impure past behind you, if you are weakened by the unholiness of bygone days, with not only your reputation, which matters little, but your character, which matters much, stained, and dwarfed, and deformed, and belittled by evil—I pray you to be heroic enough to say, "I will not transmit my own folly and my own sin to succeeding generations." I ask you, Is your life an impure life? Then, if you have no longer any care for your own soul's highest welfare; if the desire within your heart for the "whatsoever things" that are pure, and high, and noble, and of good report, has been extinguished; if the flame that trembled Godward has died upon the altar of your own heart so that you love not purity, but revel in impurity—I call upon you again from another standpoint. In committing thine own suicide thou art also committing murder. If thou hast no love for thyself, wilt thou not, O man, for the sake of the little ones glancing around in your path, in need of a friend and guide; for the sake of those children whose lives are being touched by your life every day—wilt thou not seek purity for the sake of others; and, if not, then the devoutest prayer that I can pray for thee is that God will move thee from the scene of life ere the contagion has spread too far.

There can be no more solemn and heart-searching enquiry than upon this subject of influence. Will you face this great fact, that your life is making or marring others, and you are responsible?

Says some one, "I know my own impurity, but I have received it; I know my own wrong, but it is the result of the position I have occupied in life. The bloom was brushed away before I knew its value, and I have become impure almost unconsciously." Will you hear

again the old message, full of tenderness
and God's own music? "To the house
of Israel"—that is, to the children of
faith—"there is opened a fountain for
sin and for uncleanness."

I do not mean to say that you can be
so transformed that you will stand erect
immediately in all the vigor and glory
of ideal manhood: that is impossible.
There are Christians who have been
following Christ for months, ay, for
years, who are still suffering limitations
as the result of their sin in the days
gone by. Some of us, alas! alas! will
carry to the grave the scars of the wounds
of our own mad folly in years that have
now almost faded from our memory;
but into the secret chambers of the being
there will come, to those who open wide
the door, the purifying power of the
Spirit of God. He comes to put away
transgression; to cleanse the heart; to
transmute the base and the debased into
the purified and the clean. And how?
Tell me, how can this be? It is not for
me to attempt to explain the alchemy of

the Divine work. I cannot do it. I know the laws of the Kingdom, and them I can announce to you.

I know that within the sphere where these laws operate there is abundance of cleansing, and power; but how God works I cannot tell. I cannot tell you all the mystery of the healing and the purifying work of the incoming Spirit. Canst thou tell me why the violet, hiding its head beneath the hedgerow, is of tender and beauteous hue; and why the lily growing in your garden is fleecy white? Canst thou tell me how life perfumes yon flower, so tiny that you hardly see it, and refuses to perfume the gorgeous flower that blossoms on your lawn? Hast thou no explanation for God's working? You may count the petals on the rose and tell the story of floriculture and cultivation but behind all your schemes is the touch of the Divine, the presence of God; and as thou canst not explain the painting or scenting of the flowers, and the working behind the thousand mysteries of beauty and nature, neither can I tell you how

God will come into your soul and purify
it.. What, then, is the law of His coming? It is the one simple law of absolute abandonment of self to His Kingship,
His government, and His will—that thou
mayest be what the Man of Nazareth, and
Capernaum, and the Wilderness, of the
Market Place, and Gethsemane, and Cal-
vary, intended, so that thou shalt be an
obedient child. Cease thy proud rebel-
lion against the will of God; and, committing thyself to Him, without question
as to the form and fashion of His re-
making of thee, trust His will and wondrous love, and lean on' His almighty
power.

In so doing thou shalt fulfill His law,
and out of that obedience shall come the
cleansing of thy nature; the putting away
of thy sin; the commencement of that
new life which shall exercise an influence
—pure, and strong, and high, and lovely
—which shall stretch out far beyond the
little years of thy life, into God's great
eternity.

VI

DESTINY

" And He saith unto me, Seal not up the words ot
the prophecy of this Book; for the time is at hand.
He that is unrighteous, let him do unrighteousness
yet more: and he that is filthy, let him be made
filthy yet more: and he that is righteous, let him do
righteousness yet more: and he that is holy, let him
be made holy yet more.   Behold, I come quickly,
and My reward is with Me, to render to each man
according as his work is."—Rev. xxii. 10–12.

VI

DESTINY

THE revelation of Jesus Christ, which He sent and signified to His servant John, has to do, for the most part, with things yet to come—with the end of the present age, and the ushering in of the new and golden day. The awful pronouncement contained in the central of these three verses, has special reference to the sealing of character that will take place at the advent of Jesus Christ—using that word advent in its largest sense, a sense embracing the varied aspects of His second coming. That coming of Christ will be a decisive moment to millions; fixing their character unalterably and for ever. All men wait in the purpose and counsel of God for the coming of Jesus. There have been events in history, of which we speak as remarkable and epoch-making.

In the great movement and purpose of
God, the last great event was the Incar-
nation—the first advent—and the next
will be the Return of the Lord—the second advent. The present dispensation is
one which takes its meaning and its character from the first, and will find its com-
summation and its crowning in the
second.

Let it be borne in mind that this is
not the first of the dispensations of God,
neither is it the last; and the ultimate
Divine purpose for humanity is not to be
accomplished in this dispensation of the
Spirit. There have been revealed to us,
in hints, and pictures, and symbols, and
in a few direct and forceful words, the
fact of other Divine movements, even
when the catholic Church of Jesus Christ
is completed, and the specific and special
dispensation of the Holy Spirit is at an
end. But we, of course, are interested
principally in the dispensation in which
we live; and of all peoples of the earth,
none are more deeply involved in the
conditions and movements of this age,

because it has pleased God in His government of the nations, and His selection of peoples for the carrying out of His purposes, to set upon us the choicest of His blessings, and to cause us to live in the brightest light, even of this Christian era. Therefore, while in a study such as this, other themes will suggest themselves, and other problems arise—such as the position of the heathen, dead, and living, at the coming of Christ, and the new conditions obtaining after His advent—we must turn from all of these, keeping our attention fixed upon this fact: that the verse which we have now to consider is one that has to with the present dispensation only, and specially with those people on the earth who have actually lived within its light, and therefore have known, theoretically, its method and its meaning.

At the coming of Jesus Christ, all the great forces of which we have spoken in previous discourses—the forces which counteract heredity, environment, and create right influence—will be withdrawn in the withdrawal of the Holy Spirit. Beyond that withdrawal there will be new dispensations and movements of the Divine. But we, for all practical purposes, in the consideration of the greatest of all subjects, that of our destiny, have only to do with the dispensation in which we live. Men and women are passing away from the scene of their probation; a probation spent in the light of the gospel truth. These men and women, as they pass beyond the action of these forces of the Spirit in grace, abide in exactly the same condition as that in which death finds them, until the second advent of Jesus ends this dispensation and ushers in the new.

Human life, shorter or longer, according to Divine arrangement, is a period granted to beings—the meaning of whose existence stretches far out beyond the fleeting years of that life—in which to create their own character, their own eternity; and thus each one has the power to make his own future. Let us, first of all, consider what probation is, in order that we may secondly consider how destiny grows therefrom; and in the third and last place, make an application of this consideration to our present attitude.

I

We have said that this present life of ours is the life of probation. It is well that we should understand the character of that probation. In this series of papers we have taken those verses in the writings of the apostle which hold Jesus Christ and Adam before us as being heads of the race—we have spoken of them, one as the child of disobedience, the other of obedience; transmitting the forces of their own lives to others, and each answering to environment—in one case to the true, and in the other to the false; in one case being wrecked, in the other victorious; and from these two typical cases we have drawn certain lessons which apply to ourselves.

Let it be remembered that the probation of Adam and of Christ both differed from ours. Each stood upon his own responsibility, the first man, as we believe, having a perfect start, with no tendencies inherited that would conspire to wreck his life—with the most perfect environment that man has ever known, for the creation of the tested and victorious character which God was seeking. Jesus Christ Himself embarked upon human life as a child—passing through boyhood and manhood up to maturity; but, nevertheless, because He ever dwelt in the true environment—that of the presence of God consciously known—He stood upon His own responsibility.

It is not so with us. We are born with tendencies which we did not choose, and which, propelling us, force us along the lines of action against which our better nature rebels. We are surrounded from birth with certain influences that play upon us before we understand the meaning of them, or have learned to deal with them for the making or marring of our character.

What, then, is probation to us? It is

an opportunity for the play of the forces
of grace upon characters which are
ruined from the outset. I need not stay
to discuss the awful fact of the ruin of
character at the beginning. All the mystery and the meaning of it, who shall
tell? We simply face the fact that the
tendency of human nature is to wrong,
rather than to right; that the whole
human race leans downward by the fallen
nature into which it is born, rather than
soars upward and heavenward. Yet,
side by side with that fact, is the other
fact of which we have been speaking,
that God has put into operation forces
for the re-making of character, which
are superior to anything inherited—superior to any surroundings; so that the
soul coming into living contact with
those forces may rise superior to inheritance, and overcome all contradictory environment.

Between these two sets of forces each
one of us stands; and the action of either
upon our character will depend entirely
upon our will. Amid the wreckage of

human nature there is one vital element remaining—that which lifts humanity above the level of all other creation, and makes it almost Divine—the element of will! That has not been wrecked or ruined. Man still has his will—warped, bent, inclined to evil, it may be; but remaining, so that if a man will yield himself to the forces of evil, they will work upon his life and blast his character: or, if a man will yield to the grace of God and to the power of the Holy Spirit, then those forces will make his character. Between these forces each man stands in the days of probation, having still his will, and being able to choose definitely for himself whether he will be marred by evil or made by good; whether he will become the slave of evil, losing his power of will in slavery to the evil he chooses; or, whether he will become the bond-slave of Jesus Christ, his will yielded to Kingly dominion, and so learn under that blessed constraint to love the things that make for fair and strong character.

My use of probation is described by the phrase of the text: "He that is unrighteous; he that is righteous." It cannot, in either case, be construed into meaning, "He that is in his *nature* righteous or unrighteous"; for every man enters upon life with his will between these forces, and his nature ready to respond to the one or to the other, as his will directs. It does mean that he who has refused the grace of God, and chosen deliberately the forces of evil, is the man who is unrighteous, because he has been borne along in the current to which he has committed himself. On the other hand, he who has, by an action of the will, surrendered himself to the currents of grace and the forces of purity, is rendered righteous by those very forces to which he has committed himself. My probation is not the probation of a perfect being, standing entirely alone. It is that of a man who begins life with an inheritance that hinders, and also with grace that can overcome that inheritance; with an environment that tends to degrade, and with another environment which is able to negative the force of the first: and upon the action of his will depends the issue.

II

Out of that conception of probation grows the necessity for a solemn consideration of destiny. A man's destiny is created by his use of probation. There is a moment when the Divine fiat goes forth, and probation ends—and where a man is at that moment, his character is fixed, not in degree, but in direction— and that Divine word is never spoken until I have irrevocably chosen for myself. God never draws the line across human probation until the set determination, the whole sweep of the will, has decided what that final character is to be; but the moment God draws that line, then in that chosen direction man moves on; only he that is unrighteous is to be still *more* unrighteous, and he that is righteous is to be still *more* righteous.

The one thought that I want to fix indelibly upon your minds is this—Destiny is fixed by the choice of the human will, which selects for itself its heaven or hell. Thus each one of us is building character forever. Those who are yielding to the forces around that mar the life, do so absolutely of their own free choice.

Note, then, the awful responsibility of their action. They are not choosing for the moment only, but for the morrow, and for the next day, and the next, for the years that lie ahead, and the ages that are beyond! It can all be altered now; but the day is coming when we shall no longer have the opportunity of choosing. When is that day of destiny? None can say. That secret nestles within the heart of God; only He knows the point that marks the end of man's probation.

This much is certain; probation will never end until the soul has deliberately chosen with the force of eternity; then there is no drawing back. No words more full of infinite meaning ever fell

from the lips of Jesus Christ than these,
"He that sinneth against the Holy Ghost
is in danger of eternal sin." Not, as we
have it, "eternal damnation," but "eternal sin."

It is possible for the will of man—so
magnificent is that will in its construction, so marvellous in its powers—deliberately to choose evil; and to choose
it so completely with such utter abandonment to it as to pass out into unknown ages of pain and misery. There
is no word in the Bible that exactly fits
with our word eternal. The strongest
word that we have is age-long; and no
man has any right to do other than leave
the issues of the eternities with God. In
the ages that baffle our contemplation,
there are men who will deliberately
choose evil; and the progression of evil
beyond will multiply and enlarge, and
there will be no drawing back. Destiny
is being created by the choice you are
making now. We act as though moments came to us to be smiled or sobbed
away, as the case may be, and then to

be done with forever. It is not so.
Montgomery sang truly when he sang—

> " 'Tis a mistake : time flies not,
>   He only hovers on the wing :
> Once born, the moment dies not,
>   'Tis an immortal thing."

So that the moment, here and now present, in which I choose good or evil,
purity or pollution, has its blossoming
beyond this life altogether. That is the
true view of human life. We have
treated it as though it were fleshly, carnal; as though such things were the sum
and substance. What awful madness!
Life is the workshop of eternity; the
time for making destiny; and the result
will be in accordance with the deliberate
choice of the individual will for evil or
for good.

This law of probation and destiny
operates through all the region of human
life. Do we not see it operating in lower
matters? We have an old saying that,
"The boy is father to the man." It is
perfectly true. We are but " children of

a larger growth." What the boy is—in temperament, in character, in the essentials of his life—he will be in manhood's days. At thirty, we are told, a man's habits are fixed and his character formed; and it is remarkably true in the realm of Christianity that the majority of people who are Christians were born again before they had reached thirty years of age. I do not know whether that has ever occurred to you. After that age, the number is very small as compared with the company of those who join Christ's army when the glory of youth is on their brow. It is infinitely harder to get a man who has gone over the borders of thirty years to turn to God than it is to lead a boy to Christ.

May I not turn aside and say here to every father and mother: Do not forget that. While those bairns are round your knee at home, train their thoughts in the right direction. Get the boys and girls who gather in your class, teacher, and fill the opportunity of service they present to you, as though you knew their

eternal destinies hung upon what you do
for them now; for it is possible that you
will not be able easily to change their
course at a later period. I make reverent
and thankful allowances for grace. In
some cases men have not only passed
thirty years, but have reached the allotted
span of three-score years and ten, and
yet have found the purifying grace of
God; but by comparison it is a rare oc-
currence. Let me repeat, and leave this
point with that repetition, *that the vast
majority of people who yield themselves
to Christ, do so on the sunny side of the
thirtieth milestone of their life's journey.*

So you have the law at work already.
Character is tending to permanence; and
when a man once chooses, it is difficult
for him to go back upon his choice. It
is a terrible law; but we are bound to
face it. Question the wisdom of it, if
you dare; but the fact remains, and the
fact of law is the proof of its wisdom—
for all law is of God. Every time I
choose, it becomes harder work to go
back upon my choice; and the further I

go along the line, whether of right or of wrong, the harder it is to turn back from that line. The choice made freely, now becomes a bond and a bias. I choose again in the same direction, and to-morrow it is harder to turn back than it is to-day; and so character is tending to permanence: and every hour is sealing it upon us in a way that. if we did but realize it as we ought, would appal us, and drive us to heart-searching before God.

At the coming of Jesus Christ, when we appear before Him, He will simply pronounce upon us the sentence which we have already deliberately chosen. At the judgment-bar of Jesus Christ no witnesses will be called. Why not? Because none will be needed. We do not see each other as we really are. We look at faces, and upon them we see character, to some extent; but behind the story of the faces is the story of motive, and intention, and aspiration, of determination and of will. These are things we do not see. We cannot penetrate their hiding-place. No man has

seen God at any time! No man has seen
his brother-man at any time!

When we arraign a criminal in one of
our Courts of Justice, we call our witnesses, and the judge will sum up, and
the jury will base their decision upon evidence given as to the hearing of the ear,
and the seeing of the eye. No other
judgment than that is possible. All sentences pronounced, all decisions arrived
at, are concluded upon the evidence which
comes from the seeing of the eye and the
hearing of the ear. How different the
judgment of the Eternal! Out of the old
Hebrew prophecies hear this great word:
"And He shall not judge after the sight
of His eyes, neither reprove after the
hearing of His ears." When men come
to the bar of God, they will not come
wondering what the verdict will be, or
what the sentence to be pronounced.
That verdict and sentence will not depend
upon the words spoken by witnesses.
The facts of their character will be at
once verdict and sentence. The Judge
will pronounce upon them the sentence

which they have already pronounced
upon themselves by their choice. This
principle is revealed in Matthew's account
of the judgment of the nations (see chap.
xxv.). The King will say not, "Cursed
are ye"—He has never pronounced such
a curse at all, but "Depart, ye cursed"—
cursed before the word is spoken. How
cursed? Cursed by their own choice, by
taking into their own life the forces of
evil; by surrendering themselves to the
forces that make for evil; and so render-
ing themselves insensible to the need of
the suffering "least of His brethren":
cursed, not by God, but by themselves:
literally suicides, because they have
yielded themselves to the awful forces
that mar and spoil human nature. "Come,
ye blessed": not "Blessed are ye"; but
"Ye are blessed by your own choice."
To those that choose, in the probation of
grace, the forces that make and remake
and build, God extends the sweet invita-
tion of His "Come"; but to the others
He gives the terrible command to "Depart." No witnesses will be called; for

all souls will stand naked in the presence of the Judge, and will come to the judgment-seat with sentence already decided by the deliberate choice of their own free will.

We are on our way straight to the place of judgment; and, of our own choice, deliberately move to the right or to the left. There is to be no selective separation by Divinity. There is to be selective separation by the spirits of men and women themselves. "He that is righteous, let him be righteous still; but he that is unrighteous, let him be unrighteous still." And a man is righteous because he has yielded himself to the forces of righteousness; or, he is unrighteous because he has yielded himself to the forces of unrighteousness. Thus we build our character, and create our own destiny, and prepare our own eternity.

III

In these busy days that seem to come and go with ever-increasing rapidity, and which we treat as though they were opportunities for the indulgence of carnal appetites merely, you hear men talk about "killing time." Oh, better kill anything than time; better waste anything than the moments lit as yet with the light of hope; better fritter away any wealth that happens to be in your possession, than these days overflowing with the grace and tenderness of God; for every day is an opportunity to choose, and each choice is the building of another stone into the foundation work, on which eternity will erect the structure, a structure true to the character of the foundation laid.

Is it not true that at the judgment-throne of Jesus Christ all extenuating circumstances will be taken into account? Assuredly it is! The greatest joy I have as I look upon that judgment-throne is the joy that comes from the certainty that I shall be judged, not upon testimony received, but on the essential facts of my life and choice. No single factor which has made it difficult or easy for me to choose will be left out of account. The place of my birth, my parentage, the op-

portunities granted, the use made of them
—everything will be taken into account,
and the bases of judgment for men and
women dwelling in these lands of privi-
lege, and for those living in the heart of
heathen countries, will be the same in
this sense, that God will judge men right-
eously and justly, according to the opportunities they have had. It is that very
identity of eternal justice which will dif-
ferentiate between the responsibilities of
the one class and of the other. God will
not expect from that man who has never
heard the sound of Jesus' name, the
same report of himself at the Great White
Throne as He will from you, who have
been familiar with Him. Certainly, extenuating circumstances will be taken into
account; but, remember this: Jesus said,
speaking of the Spirit, "When He is
come, He will convict the world in respect of sin, and of righteousness, and of
judgment." Now, that is one of the
phrases which is perpetually misquoted.
Almost every one puts in two words
which rob it of its force and meaning.

People say, "Of righteousness, and of judgment *to come.*"

The judgment of which He spoke was not *to come*, but judgment accomplished: "The prince of this world *is* judged." When, therefore, we speak of this as the day of grace, let us remember, it is the day of grace because judgment is pronounced already upon evil, by the victory of Jesus. If we deliberately make choice of evil, then must we share the judgment passed upon evil now, at the Great White Throne, and forever; but if we choose to yield to the authority of the Vanquisher of evil, then are we lifted into the sphere of His resurrection life, which is the life of absolute victory over all the forces that are against us.

How does this affect the plea of extenuating circumstances? If a man is to set up this plea he must apply it, not to half the case, but to the whole; not merely to the forces that were against, but also to those which were for him.

The man who pleads extenuating circumstances, and who continues in his wrongdoing because of that plea, by that very action makes it impossible that those extenuating circumstances should be allowed. What would you say of a man who, tempted to the breaking of the law of the land, says, "I am driven to this crime; it will be all right, the judge will take into account the extenuating circumstances, and, therefore, I will do it"? The judge would say, "By that deliberate choice, you denied the extenuating circumstances; for had they been, the act would have been sudden and swift, and repented of." He that chooses deliberately to do wrong, because of excuses he may be able to plead, proves there was no necessity for the wrongful act. The man who has time to calculate upon extenuating circumstances has more than time to put himself into treaty and contact with the forces of grace, which are superior to all such circumstances. God can excuse no man who, pleading excuses in order that he may do these evil things, does not tell the whole story of the case. The strict justice that will make all allowance, also demands that we shall make full use of the forces that God has put into operation for us, and which lie close to our hand.

There is no thought of the future so full of solemn heart-searching power as this of permanence of character. Do you choose impurity in any of its forms? Then you choose it, not for to-day, but forever. Do you choose purity at any cost? Then you choose it, not for to-day, but forever. The issue of this momentous choice lies beyond all time and all scenes that fade. How this lifts my present life into the most lurid and awful light! What am I here for? I am here that I may prepare for all that lies beyond. What does to-morrow bring to me? Business hours, do you say? Opportunities for hard work, and beyond that, rest? Nay, verily: to-morrow brings, if its light shall dawn, further hours to choose, not for to-day, but forever. I choose as I stand here in the pulpit. You choose as you sit in the pews. And our choice does not end with the selection of this or of that, it runs out into the eternities.

The ultimate issue of every action of every day is not what it seems to be in the view of men and women whose vision is bounded by the horizon of probational life; but the true issue of these doings of to-day is the character that exists hereafter. Have I, then, to build my own character, to construct my own eternity, to make for myself my heaven or my hell? Assuredly I have! Then how long will God give me in which to do it? How long will He allow me in which to build and create that destiny? Not an hour; not a moment. *Now* is the only word that God speaks to human souls. "But," you say, "I cannot build character in an hour; I cannot undo what has been done in the past in a moment. How can I?" *Now!* It is here to undo or do; to break down or to build up. In God's now, ever present with you, never far away, this moment you can *will*. Beyond that *you* can do nothing. But in the plan of God that is enough! You will, and force responds to your will. You say, "I will take the way of sin"; and immediately all the disintegrating forces of sin begin to play with your moral fibre and rob you of the force to will anything but that which you have now " willed." Or, you say, "I will be righteous," and then the stronger forces of grace begin their work upon you; to build up where you have broken down; to repair the ruined structure of your character: and so every moment is a moment in which I am to will, and every crisis is a crisis in which I am to will; and to my will respond forces of evil or forces of righteousness, according to the way I will.

How, then, shall we "will"? There, on the one hand, stretches the path— easy and flowery and filled with music, so men tell us—a path that needs no heroism. If I will that, then that is the issue as well as the crisis: and away to the other side stretches the path that is rough and thorny—so men tell us—the path that demands nerve, and is shadowed with conflict and strife. If I will that, then that is the issue as well as the crisis. But that is not the true story of either of these paths. I have simply for a moment taken the popular conception of them. Hear another story of this path, so flowery and radiant with light and color, and vibrating with music. "The way of transgressors is hard"—not the *end* of it, but the *way* itself. Hunger, dissatisfaction, disappointments, are its concomitants; and the soul is never at rest. Well, if I choose it, *that is the issue as well as the crisis.* What of this other path? It is the path of perfect peace, where harmony is substituted for strife, and the storms are swallowed up in peace, "the peace of God which passeth all understanding"; and if I will that, *that is the issue as well as the crisis.* The one leads to the everlasting hunger, and the other to the everlasting rest.

God, in Christ, bends over man in infinite pity—over the man whom He has created in His own image, endowing him with power to will, and He says,

"Wilt thou be made whole?" and I turn my back to the allurements of this side that leads to evil and to hunger, and I say, " O Nazarene, Thou hast conquered by an infinitude of love; and if out of the wreckage of my life Thou canst create character that abides, I give myself to Thee, and I 'will' to follow Thee." That path leads right on to the eternal rest. I choose in the pulpit; and you cannot help me. You must choose in the pew; and I cannot help you. God help preacher and people alike to choose aright.